HIDE-AND-SEEK WITH GOD

STORIES BY
Mary Ann Moore

Skinner House Books
Boston, Massachusetts

Copyright © 1994 by Mary Ann Moore.
Cover illustration copyright © 1994 by Martha Frances Patton.
All rights reserved.

Published by Skinner House Books, an imprint of the Unitarian Universalist Association,
25 Beacon Street, Boston, MA 02108.

ISBN 1-55896-277-8

10 9 8 7 6 5 4   / 99 98 97

Printed in the United States of America.

Acknowledgments

I am deeply aware that nothing is totally my own creation. So many people's thoughts, concerns, and feelings become a part of me that they often feel like mine, but I know they aren't mine alone. The stories in this book are like that. They are mine, but they also belong to all those people from the beginning of time whom I never knew and to all the people I know today who have wondered about ultimate things. This especially includes the teachers and children who field-tested these stories. I am grateful to them all.

In addition, I am especially thankful for two people who contributed to the development of these stories. One is Frances Patton, who worked with me every step of the way as the stories came to be. I would write a story; she would hear it and share her thoughts about it. I would rewrite the story, and she would comment again. Her understanding of young children, her concern for feminist images, and her spirituality are all present in these stories.

The second person is my husband, Jim Moore, who also read and critiqued each story. I very much appreciate his scientific outlook, his ability to help me unravel cumbersome sentences, and his basic sensibleness. Jim has given me every kind of encouragement and support for taking on such a project.

I am truly appreciative of the contributions of both Frances and Jim.

CONTENTS

Introduction

When we say the word "God," we move out of our everyday way of speaking into a special form of religious communication. It lets us talk about ultimate concerns and helps us to understand and express answers to such universal questions as:

- What is the source of creation?
- What force causes the changes of birth, growth, and death?
- What happens after death?
- How can we explain the tragedies of life?
- Why do suffering and evil exist?
- What is the source of healing and forgiveness?
- What is the formula for an ethical life?
- How can justice, peace, and compassion be achieved?

• What gives life positive meaning?

Religious communication systems weave the answers to such questions into a larger vision that helps us understand ultimate reality, ultimate values, and ultimate mystery. But the answers inevitably reveal paradoxes, as well.

A communication system that uses symbols with many levels of meaning allows us to express our understanding of ultimate concerns in a more satisfying way than a system based on logic alone. Though such systems may employ reason and analysis, usually that kind of thinking is used to examine the more primary images, symbols, and metaphors of a religion. These images may take the form of myths and poetry, art and music, rituals and dance, meditation or prayers, sounds and silence. Because the forms of these images are often much more than words, the term "religious communication system" seems more appropriate than "religious language," though the latter is often used.

In religious communication systems, the word "God" is usually central; it is what Gordon Kaufman calls an anchor-symbol. When considering the word "God," it is important to remember several things. First, "God" is the English word generally used by people in monotheistic western traditions; other languages have similar words, such as *Gott, Dios,* or *Allah.* Those who say "God" and those who say "*Dios*" may mean more or less the same thing. On the other hand, people who use the English word "God" may have very different interpretations among themselves. Secondly, people from some of the world's other religions use words such as *Shakti, Buddha, Wakan Tanka,* and *Mawu* to speak of ultimate reality, value, and mystery. These words not only have different sounds but may indicate many different concepts. Finally, there are people who use *Spirit, Goddess, Life,* or *Love* to refer to what many people mean by "God."

The stories in this book use "God" in the sense of Kaufman's anchor-symbol for several reasons. It has traditionally been the English word used to answer ultimate questions. As our answers change, the use of "God" maintains an important continuity. The use of this word also provides a common starting place for dialogue with others about ultimate questions. Finally, the word "God" does not have another more concrete meaning embedded in its etymology, as, for example, "life" and "love" do. Though some feel that "God" connotes a male deity, it does not have the absolute sense of gender that "Goddess" does. Hopefully, a new generation can grow up understanding God to mean both male and female, along with a variety of other qualities.

Some people who use "God" to express their understanding of ultimate concerns are bothered by the images used to portray the concept of God. Some are uncomfortable with God images suggesting that God is like a person. For them, the idea of an anthropomorphic God seems too simplistic or suggests that there is a divine being who is totally removed from humans and who has absolute authority over them.

However, it is possible to understand an anthropomorphic God in a different way. If God stands for an ultimate reality or value within us, and we wish to express ideas about that God in a story, it is appropriate for God to be like a person because we are persons. In most of these stories, when God speaks like a person and engages the children as a person would, it is clear that God is found within persons, in dreams, in forgiveness, in caring, in love, and so on. The theology in these stories proposes that God is both immanent (within us) and transcendent (something greater than ourselves). That paradox can be nicely conveyed by an anthropomorphic God in a myth-like story. What matters most is that the anthropomorphic image depicts a God who is compatible with one's beliefs about ultimate concerns. Is the personified God one who expects total obedience, who is violent, and who is only male? Or is God one who works in a cooperative way with people, who is surprised by events in the universe, who wants peace and forgiveness, and who can be male or female? The portrayal of values, not the anthropomorphism, is the crucial issue.

Another issue of concern is the image of a judgmental God—one who judges actions to be right or wrong and people to be good or evil. People concerned with this issue do not accept images of a God who is totally different from us and who makes absolute decisions about right and wrong. However, these same people find that they make their own judgments about actions and people and believe that to be necessary. How can we resolve this conflict of attitudes? Some don't. They accept the idea of human judgment but reject any concept of God as a judge. Others consider the following.

First, keep in mind that God can symbolize both something within us and something greater than ourselves. Second, keep in mind that images of God interweave our understandings of what is (ultimate reality) and what we believe ought to be (ultimate value), as well as mystery. Now, imagine an optical illusion, such as a box which changes its orientation as your perspective on it shifts. The image you see depends on how your viewing clicks into place. Look at things from the view of ultimate reality and accept what is; look at things from the view of ultimate values and strive to bring them about. Sprinkle both from time to time with mystery. God is both what is and what ought to be; God both accepts and exhorts. As with the issue of anthropomorphism, what matters is not the imaging that includes "oughts," but the kind of judgments and the methods used to convey them.

These stories offer a pattern, a tapestry, a nexus of God images reflecting the belief that ultimate reality is an interdependent oneness; that ultimate values are love and the worth of each person; and that both are tempered by ultimate mystery.

Oneness is the source of the diversity of forces we find, such as female and male, birth and death, light and dark, silence and sound. The oneness holds these forces together in an interrelated and interdependent whole. If we use the word "God" to symbolize ultimate reality, then God can be understood as a oneness that takes many different forms.

Love and worth permeate all that is, and convey an inherent value which is universal to all that is. This sense of the dignity of all is a source of justice and peace, compassion and forgiveness, respect for the earth, and joy. If we use the word "God" to symbolize ultimate value, then God can be thought of as love and worth that takes many different forms.

Mystery weaves in and out of all our beliefs about oneness and love and worth. Mystery requires freedom and openness; it evokes wonder, surprise, and awe. It implies an understanding that there are many paths, that God has many names or none at all, that hearing different views can be helpful, and that change, at times, reflects truth best. If we use the word "God" to symbolize ultimate mystery, then God can be thought of as mystery that takes many different forms.

It is important to remember that oneness, love, worth, and mystery in their many forms are totally interwoven. Although we can focus on one at a given time, the others are always there in the background.

The stories in this collection offer young children the beginnings of a religious language for talking about God as they strive to find answers to universal religious questions and ways to express them. They are seeds to be sown, scattering metaphors, images, and symbols, connecting the word "God" to a pattern of beliefs about ultimate reality, value, and mystery.

Children from four to eight years old are especially receptive to such seeds. This is a period of major developmental transformation: a movement from being immersed in the oneness of self and the world to a sense of separateness and individuality. Children undergoing these changes still intuit the sense of connectedness which is at the heart of spirituality and which, in one way, is ineffable. Yet they are also gaining language skills and conceptual abilities that require speaking of things as individual entities.

Faith-development theorist Jim Fowler writes that children at this stage "can be powerfully and permanently influenced by examples, moods, actions and stories of the visible faith of primally related adults." He goes on to say, "imagination in this stage is extremely productive of long-lasting images and feelings (positive and negative) that later, more stable and self-reflective valuing and thinking will have to order and sort out. . . . The gift or emergent strength of this stage is the birth of imagination, the ability to unify and grasp the experience-world in powerful images and as presented in stories that register the child's intuitive understandings and feelings toward the ultimate conditions of existence."

These stories were written as the core of a church-school curriculum that provided opportunities for concrete and sensual exploration of the images and metaphors in the stories. Adults who read these stories to girls and boys may wish to make connections to concepts the children already know and to experiences they have had. Understanding a child well makes it possible to relate the story to her or his interests and understandings in a way that often cannot happen in a group setting.

These stories were also meant to be the center of a process in which children first have a chance to express what they already know and believe. Then the story with new ideas is presented. Finally, there are opportunities for the children to integrate their own thoughts and feelings, keeping some ideas and rejecting others. I hope that adults who read these stories to children will do so in that spirit.

Mary Ann Moore
Sudbury, Massachusetts
November, 1993

HIDE-AND-SEEK WITH GOD

Once upon a time God said, "I'm bored because I don't have anything to do. I want to play with my friends." And because God is God, as soon as the words were spoken, God's friends were there. When God saw them all gathered, God said, "I've been bored because I haven't had anything to do. Let's play something."

"Good idea," said God's friends, "What shall we play?"

God thought for a minute and then said, "I know, let's play hide-and-seek!"

The friends all said, "Yeay!" They knew that hide-and-seek with God was always exciting and different because God was the one who hid and God always thought of wonderful places to hide.

God's friends closed their eyes tight and counted to ten. When they opened their eyes, God wasn't there anymore. So they all went off to look for God.

One friend decided to look close on the earth and soon came to a meadow. As he was searching, he stopped to admire the tender new sprouts of green grass pushing their way up toward the sun. As he bent over to look more closely at the tender green, he realized there was something special and amazing and wonderful about it. So he jumped up and ran back to home base, calling out, "I found God! God is green and growing. I found God in the grass!"

Another one of God's friends decided to look for God in the night. She watched the sun go down, and heard the work-a-day noises stop, and saw the lights in the houses go out. As it got darker and the peaceful night wrapped itself around her, she listened very hard, and then she realized there was something special and amazing and wonderful about it. And when it was so still that she could see and hear nothing at all, she suddenly jumped up and ran to home base, calling out, "I found God! God is dark and peaceful. I found God in the night!"

A third friend looked on the earth and felt the mystery of the grass growing toward the sun. He stayed and watched the night come on, and he felt the mystery of the darkness and the stars. He thought to himself, "These mysteries are special and amazing and wonderful." But when he finally came back to home base, he said, "I found wonderful mysteries but I'm not sure if I want to call them God."

A fourth friend decided to look for God where people were. He joined a group of people going home from work and went with them into the store where they bought food. He went with them back out on the street as they started for their homes. He was with them when someone came up and said, "Please, I'm very hungry. Could you share a little food with me?" The people readily agreed and as he watched them share, he realized there was something special and amazing and wonderful about those people. He turned around and ran to home base, calling out, "I found God! God is love and sharing. I found God in people who care for others!"

Finally, two more of God's friends, a boy and a girl, decided to look for God together. After a time, they came to a house and decided to look for God in the house. In the house they saw a room, and they looked for God in the room. In the room they saw a mirror, and they looked for God in the mirror. As they looked into the mirror, they realized there was something special and amazing and wonderful being reflected in it. They turned around and ran to home base, calling out, "We found God! We found God in us!"

At this God appeared again and said, "I had so much fun! Weren't those good hiding places? Some of you found me, others weren't sure, and others are still looking. That's OK because the most important thing is just to play the game. Let's do it again! I'm sure I can think of some other good hiding places." And they all called out, "Olly, olly, oxen free, free, free!" And the game started all over again.

GOD HAS MANY NAMES

Once upon a time, a girl and a boy played with each other and argued with each other. Sometimes they argued about who could swing the highest, and sometimes they argued about whose cookie was the biggest. One time, though, they were arguing about God's real name.

The girl said, "God's real name is Mother of Us All."

The boy said, "No it isn't, God's real name is Father in Heaven."

"No," the girl said. "It's Mother."

"It is not," the boy said. "It's Father."

"I have an idea," said the girl. "Let's go find God and ask her what her real name is. Then we'll know for sure and you'll see I'm right."

"OK," agreed the boy. "I think that's a very good idea because when we find God, he will tell you that his real name is Father."

So the boy and the girl set off to find God, even though both of them admitted they were a bit afraid to go far from home and they might be afraid to talk to God. After they had gone some distance, they met people carrying food home from the market. They said to the people, "We are looking for God so that we can find out what God's real name is."

One of the people said, "I think if you go straight ahead down that road you will find God, but I can tell you that God's real name is The Giver of Life." The children thanked the people but told them that they still wanted to ask God themselves. The people offered the children some bread and fruit, and they continued on.

They came to a river where people were fishing from a boat, and they asked them where they could find God so that they could find out God's real name. The people told them they would have to cross the river to find God, but one of the people said, "You don't have to go across because we know God's real name. It is The Hidden One. But if you still want to go on, we will give you a ride to the other side of the river." The children thanked them and crossed the river, continuing on.

The boy and the girl were beginning to get tired as they approached another group of people in a grove of trees. "We want to find out God's real name. Do you know where we can find God?" the girl and boy asked.

"You may find God if you go a little deeper into the forest," one of the people replied. "But it isn't necessary. I can tell you God's real name. It is Protector."

"We still want to find out for ourselves," the children said.

"Well, take these blankets for your journey," the people replied. The children thanked them and traveled on deeper into the forest.

Night came. The girl and the boy ate the bread and fruit, then lay down on the blankets to sleep. When morning came, just as the sun was peeping through the trees, they heard a kindly voice say, "I understand that there are children here who want to know my real name."

"That's right. We do!" cried the girl and boy together. "Are you afraid?" the girl whispered.

"No," said the boy. "Are you?"

"I'm not, either," the girl said. "God sounds friendly."

"Well, what do you think my real name is?" asked God.

"I think it is Mother of All," said the girl.

"And so it is!" said God.

"See," the girl said happily to the boy. "I was right!"

"Well," the boy said, disappointed. "I thought it was Father in Heaven."

"And so it is!" God said again.

"See," said the boy, happy now. "I was right!"

"Wait a minute," the girl said, thinking hard. "How can we both be right? And what about those people we met on our trip who said your name was Giver of Life and Hidden One and Protector—what about them?"

"They are right, too," said God.

"But how can you have more than one real name?" asked the boy. "Doesn't one of them have to be the real name, the only right name?"

"No," said God, "I have many names. Some people say I have ninety-nine names and some people say I have thousands of names."

"What are some of those ninety-nine names?" the girl asked.

"Well, Giver of Life, Hidden One, and Protector are three of them," God replied. "Some others are The Truth, The Creator, and The Loving One, and, of course, the one-hundredth name is Allah."

"What are some of the thousands of names?" asked the boy.

"Mother of All, Father in Heaven, *Shiva*, The Great Spirit, Gaia. Any of these names is my real name if the person who calls me it does so with a loving heart," God explained.

"Well, my heart feels loving when I call you Mother of All," said the girl.

"And my heart feels loving when I call you Father in Heaven," said the boy.

"Then Mother of All is my real name for you," God said to the girl. "And Father in Heaven is my real name for you," God said to the boy.

The girl and the boy thanked God for helping them to understand. As they went home, they argued about who had been the bravest. But they didn't argue anymore about God's real name.

THE ONE GREAT WEB OF LIFE

Once there was a boy who wondered about things. He had been told that everything in the world was part of God's Oneness, but when he looked around him he saw many different things: the sun and moon, trees and rivers, houses and cars, plants and animals, and people. He just couldn't understand how all these different things could be a Oneness.

One summer day this boy was playing outside. After a time he got tired and he lay down on the grass to rest. As he lay there, looking up at the clouds, he thought again about how the clouds and the grass and even he could all be part of a Oneness. Just then he noticed a spider dropping down from the branch of a nearby bush. Closer and closer to him she came, on a tiny silk thread that she spun out of the back of her body. He couldn't believe his ears when the spider said to him, "So you are wondering how all the different things in the world can be part of God's Oneness. Would you like me to help you to understand?"

The boy gulped, and for a minute he couldn't even say anything. He was amazed that the spider could speak and even more amazed that she knew what he was thinking. "Can you really tell me?" he asked. The spider said, "I won't tell you with words, but I will show you. Watch me!"

And the spider began to spin more of the silky threads out of her body and to weave them into a web. First she made a bridge from one bush to another. Next she decided where the center of the web would be, and from that center she made connections to other parts of the bushes. Finally the spider went back into the center and started out again, this time circling around and around, crisscrossing over and over the framework, working her way from the center out to the edges until the web was done.

Proud of her creation, she said, "Do you like my web?"

"Oh, yes, it's wonderful!" the boy replied.

"Does it give you any ideas about how all the different things in the world are part of the Oneness?"

"Well," thought the boy. "First there was just you and now there are all these pretty threads in a nice crisscrossy design. The threads are different from you but they came out of you, so they must be a part of you, too."

"That's very good," replied the spider. "I can see you are a very good thinker."

"And," the boy went on, "all the threads are connected to each other."

"Yes," said the spider. "And, just like the web, all the different things in the world come from God, and even though there are many different things, they are still all connected to each other. But there's more. Take that stick there and move just one part of the web, any part, and see what happens."

The boy picked up the stick and gently jiggled one of the outer threads.

"What happened?" asked the spider.

"It moved."

"Just the part you touched?"

"No," said the boy. "The whole web moved."

"That's right. Nothing happens on one part of the web that the rest of the web doesn't feel. I always keep one foot on some part of the web and if anything touches it, anywhere, I know it. In the same way, when something happens to one of the things in the One Great Web of Life, somehow or other it happens to everything else."

The boy wondered about this for a while and then said, "I can see the threads on your web touching each other but I can't see all the things in the world touching each other."

"That's true," said the spider. "The crisscrosses on the One Great

Web of Life are not as easy to see as the ones on my web, but they are there, just the same. You have to use your imagination to see them. Some people call that your inner eye. Close your eyes for a minute. Imagine you see those bean seeds you planted a while ago. What did they connect with so that they could grow?"

The boy closed his eyes and thought of the seeds. He remembered putting them in soil from the earth, he remembered placing them so the sun could shine on them, and he remembered watering them. "I think they touched the earth, the sun, the water, and they even touched me."

"Now you're beginning to understand," said the spider. "To see the crisscrosses on my web you can use your regular eyes. To see the Oneness of the Great Web of Life you have to use your inner eye or your imagination."

"To see the Oneness of the Great Web of Life I have to use my inner eye," repeated the boy. Seeing that the boy was beginning to understand, the spider crawled quietly away on one of her threads to rest, and the boy, who had rested enough, got up to play again.

God Is Like the Mother of All

In the beginning God just was. After a time she said to herself, "I am tired of just being. I want to do something." So the Power in her began to move. She wiggled and squirmed and wished very hard, and suddenly out she went, out and out and out.

After a time, some parts of her began to gather back together, swirling and twirling until they formed a round, brown ball spinning through space. For a time, God was happy.

But after some time went by, she said to herself, "I'm tired of just being a round, brown ball. I want to do something more." So the Power in her began to move. She wiggled and squirmed and wished very hard, and she brought forth mountains and lowlands.

After her efforts she thought to herself, "That was really hard work. I don't have anyone to help me. I never realized it before, but I'm very lonely." Then she brought forth great tears of sadness, and they flooded out onto the lowlands, forming oceans and lakes. All these watery places were a lovely blue color, and for a time God was happy.

More time went by, and she said to herself, "I like my roundness. I like my mountains and lowlands. I especially like the lovely, watery blue places that my tears have made, but I want to do something more." So the Power in her began to move. She wiggled and squirmed and wished very hard, and in places where there was water, she brought forth green plants. Some stayed low to the ground, and others grew so tall they seemed to reach for the top of the sky, but all had roots deep inside her. For a while God was happy.

But again after a time she said to herself, "I like my roundness and my mountains and my blue watery places and my green plants, but I still want to do something more." So the Power in her began to move. She wiggled and squirmed and wished very hard, and she brought forth animals that could move around on their own. Simple little animals became fancier and fancier until the seas were full of fish, the land was full of reptiles and mammals, and birds flew through the air everywhere. Again God was happy with herself.

But after another long time she said to herself, "I like my roundness, my mountains, my plants, and my animals, but I want to do one thing more. I am still lonely, and I have brought forth so much that I cannot care for it all. I need companions who will keep me company and help me." So the Power in her began to move again. She wiggled and squirmed and she squirmed and wiggled and she wished extremely hard, and finally she brought forth human beings, a woman and a man.

"I have brought you forth from myself to be my helpers," said God. "The mountains, the waters, the plants, and the animals all need to be looked after. I want you to help me care for them. In return, they and I will give you what you need for a good life. Can you think of anything more that you need?"

The woman and the man thought for a while. Then they said, "We want for there to be more of us. We don't think only two of us can give you all the help you need." So God gave them part of her power—the power to bring forth a child. After a time their child came to them from the woman's body. And the child called the man Father, and the child called the woman Mother, and the man and woman called the child Beloved One.

The man and the woman were very happy, and they felt grateful to God for giving them so much. They wanted to give her something back. They said, "We know you are the source of everything, but can you think of anything you need?"

God thought for a long time and finally said, "It is true that I am the source of all things, but in spite of that there is one thing I lack. I don't have a name. Just as your child has named you and you have named your child, I want you to give me a name."

So the power in the woman and the man began to move. They

wiggled and squirmed and wished very hard, and finally they said to God, "We name you Mother of All, because just as the woman brought forth our child from her body, so you brought forth everything that is from your body."

Before long there were more children, and those children had children, and the children's children had children, and soon there were many, many people to help. And God, who was now called Mother of All, was very, very happy.

GOD IS LIKE A FATHER

As Jesus was growing up he learned many things about God. He learned that God cared about what happened to people, and he learned that God wanted people to care about each other. He also learned that he could talk with God, and when he talked to God he called him Father. After Jesus grew up, he traveled around the countryside, meeting many people and telling them how God wanted them to care for each other.

One time a large group of people gathered around Jesus. One of them came forward and said, "Jesus, I want to do the things that God wants me to do, but sometimes it is hard to know what I am supposed to do. God has given us many rules to follow, such as don't steal, don't lie, and don't hurt others. But sometimes it is hard to remember all the rules. Can you tell me an easy way to remember what God wants me to do?"

Jesus said to God, "Father, one of your children wants to know a way to remember all the things you want your people to do. What shall I say?"

God answered, "Tell them that all those rules really mean one simple thing: Love each other." So that was what Jesus told them.

But one of the people said to Jesus, "Must we love everybody, even people who are different from us?"

Jesus spoke to God again, saying, "Father, they want to know if they must love people who are different."

God answered, "Tell them that every one of them is different and special, but they are all my children and I love each one and I want them to love each other." So that was what Jesus told them.

The people who came to talk with Jesus noticed that he talked to God. They asked him to teach them how to talk with God. So Jesus spoke to God again and said, "Father, your children want to know how to talk with you. What shall I tell them?"

God answered, "Tell them to talk with me in prayer." So that was what Jesus did. He taught the people a prayer like this one:

Father, blessed is your name.
May we learn to love each other.
May a world of love come to be.
Give us this day the things we need,

And forgive us for the wrong things we do,
As we will forgive others.
Keep us safe from evil.
Amen.

Being With God In Prayer

Once there was a child who had a problem: All of her friends would climb up to the top of the highest slide on the playground and slide down. But even though she liked to slide on the smaller slide, she was afraid to go up to the top of the highest slide. And there was more to the problem. Her friends sometimes teased her because she wouldn't slide down the highest slide. Sometimes they called her "a baby."

Whenever she thought about this problem she felt very tight inside and didn't want to talk about it. When her friends called her a baby, she said, "No, I'm not. I just like the smaller slide better." But she was starting to notice how exciting it looked to go down the big slide, and how much fun her friends were having, and she wished that she could do it, too. But she still was afraid.

She wanted to explain to someone how she felt, but she didn't know who to talk to. One day, when she was visiting her grandmother by herself, she said, "Grandmother, I want to talk to somebody about a problem, but not my friends, or my teachers, or my parents." Her grandmother said, "Well, you certainly can share it with me, if you want to, or you could share it with God in a prayer."

"Share it with God in a prayer!" the girl replied. "How do you do that? Do you have to use special words, like Amen?"

"No," her grandmother explained. "You can just talk as you would with anyone, or you can sit quietly and just think and feel."

"Don't you have to go to a special place to pray, like church?" the girl asked.

"No, you can be with God anywhere, although church is a good place."

"I saw some people pray once, and they bowed their heads and put their hands in a special way. Do you have to do those things?"

"Not at all," her grandmother reassured her. "Though bowing your head or closing your eyes or holding your hands together and near your heart is sometimes helpful. You can use any words, you can be anywhere and you can have your body anyway that is comfortable for you. But there are three things you must remember when you pray."

"What are they?" the girl asked.

"The first is that when you share something with God, you also have to listen. The second is that sometimes you have to wait to hear God answer. And the third is that God may surprise you."

"Thank you, Grandmother," the girl said as she hugged her. "I'm going to try sharing my problem with God, and I will remember what you told me."

When the girl went home, she went into her bedroom, sat comfortably on her bed, and said, "Hi, God. I have a problem I want to share with you." Then she told God all about the high slide and the teasing, and how she wished she could get brave enough to go down the slide.

She waited quietly, listening. As she listened she heard some words going around in her head: "Sliding—so high—scared—climbing—fun." As she listened she heard some more words: "You go up the small slide—the big slide is just a few more steps—once you were afraid to let go in the water and swim, but all of a sudden one day you did it—when you are ready—you can do it." She wondered, "Is that God helping me with my problem?"

That night as she slept, she had a dream. She saw a great huge slide that went all the way up into the clouds, and she was climbing up the steps of the slide with God following behind her. When she got to the top, she sat down and she heard God say, "Go!" And then, with a cry of "Here I go!" she pushed off and slid all the way back to earth, and God did, too. It was so exciting and wonderful that right away she did it again. When she woke up she remembered her dream and wondered, "Was God really there, in my dream?"

27

For several days she shared her problem with God, and she dreamed at night, and she went to school and looked at the high slide, but she still went down the small one. Then one day, a boy who was sliding with her on the small slide said, "I want to go down the big slide but I'm afraid to do it by myself. Would you come over and climb up right behind me? If you were there with me I don't think I'd be so afraid."

"Sure," the girl said, surprising herself. "I'll come with you."

So they went to the big slide. The boy started climbing up and the girl climbed right behind him. When he got to the top, he sat down very carefully and then off he went, down, down the slide. "I did it!" he yelled out. "Because you were there and I knew I wouldn't fall!"

All this time the girl had not been thinking about how high the slide was because she was thinking about helping the boy. Now she saw she was almost to the top. She just had one more step to go and she wasn't afraid—well, not very much. So she climbed up the last step, sat down, and heard a voice within her saying, "Go, you can do it!" Down she went, sucking in her breath with the thrill of it. And then the boy and the girl went up and down the slide over and over again.

That night in her room, the girl said to God, "It is good to be with you. I had to listen hard and I had to wait, but you were with me. And you surely did surprise me today! I didn't know I was ready, but I guess you did. Thanks, God—and oh, yes, Amen."

GOD IS LIKE A COMPASSIONATE DEER

Once there was a very special deer. You would notice this deer right away because of its three-pointed antlers, the long hair at its throat, and its beautiful coloring. It was intelligent and could run swiftly and leap great distances, but it was also tender and loving. This wonderful deer lived in a very deep forest, far away from towns and people.

One day, the king decided to go hunting, and he and his followers set out into the forest on their horses. The king, of course, rode the fastest horse and he became so excited at chasing the animals and trying out his bow and arrow that, without knowing it, he soon left the others behind and entered the deepest part of the woods.

All of a sudden the king saw the wonderful, special deer. He knew that this was the deer he wanted to shoot. He strung his bow and urged his horse to gallop swiftly after the deer. The Great Deer saw him coming and took off as fast as lightning. As he was fleeing, the deer came to a wide ditch, which he was easily able to leap across to safety on the other side. The king's horse, however, knew he could not jump that far, so when he came to the edge he stopped suddenly and the king was thrown off the horse and into the deep ravine.

The Great Deer, not hearing sounds behind him anymore, looked back. He saw the riderless horse standing at the edge of the ravine and realized what must have happened to the king. Now we could understand if the deer had kept on running, happy not to be chased anymore. Instead, the Great Deer thought not of himself, but of the king who might be injured and needing help. The deer said to himself, "The king has been used to a royal life with someone always there to help him with everything. Now he may be lying hurt and in pain, and there is no one else to help. I cannot leave him there alone."

So the Great Deer went back and looked over the rim of the ravine. Below him he saw the king lying on the ground with his royal clothing all torn and dusty. Full of compassion for the king, the deer no longer thought of him as an enemy, but felt only sympathy and concern for him. Tears came to the deer's eyes and he said to the king, "I hope your pain is not too great. Do you think you have broken any bones? Though I am only a creature of the woods, I have the power to rescue you. Just tell me if you wish me to help you."

The king was surprised to hear the deer speak, and even more amazed that the one he had intended to kill was now caring about him. The king felt ashamed and thought to himself, "Though he bears the shape of an animal, I am the one who is the real beast." The king answered the deer, "My armor protected me when I fell, so my injuries are not too great. I can bear the pain of my body; worse, though, is the pain I feel knowing that I was trying to kill you. But if you still want to help, I accept your offer."

The Great Deer was happy that the king would let him help. He leaped down into the ravine and said, "Mount on my back, Your Majesty, and hold on tight." This the king did, and the deer crouched down and then sprung upward, bringing them both to the top. He helped the king back onto his horse and explained how to get out of the forest.

The king, full of gratitude, said, "My life is yours, O Great and Compassionate Deer. I will do anything for you. Why don't you come with me and live in my palace and I will give you everything you want. Don't stay in these woods, where someone else might come and kill you."

But the Great Deer answered the king, "I do not seek the pleasures of your palace, O King; I am content to live here in the forest. However, if you truly wish to help me, stop your hunting. I will have all I want if you and others no longer wish to harm any deer, or other animals, or birds, or insects. All we want is to be left in peace in this beautiful place."

The king agreed readily and then set off for his home, now full of love and compassion for all creatures.

THINGS GOD MADE FOR JOY

In the beginning, God was very serious as she brought the world into being. "This is very important work," she said to herself, "and I must think very carefully about what I am creating."

First she made the light and the dark. "Light and dark are very important," she said. "We need light so we can see to work. We need dark so we can rest."

Then she made the earth and the sky. "Earth and sky are very important," she said. "We need the earth so we can feel at home. We need the sky so we can look up and away."

Next she made living plants and creatures. "Plants and animals are very important," she said, "They will help with food and clothing and houses."

Then she made women and men. "Human beings are very important," she said. "They will be companions for me and will help me with the work of the world." And then she rested from all that very important work.

After she rested, she looked around at all she had made and saw how important it was, but somehow she wasn't completely happy about it. She said to herself, "I know I should be very proud of all this important work—light and dark, earth and sky, plants and animals, and people—and I am. Still, it all seems just too serious. Something is missing. What is it that is missing?"

She thought for a while, and then she knew. "Besides all the serious, important things in my world, there should be some things that are just for fun. I'm going to create some things for the world that are just for fun!"

So God got busy again. She said, "I made the light and dark, and they are serious and important, but I think I'll just play around with them for the fun of it." She started tossing them up and mixing and matching them, and suddenly there was a shimmering, bright yellow and a deep, powerful red and one of her favorites: a cheerful, vibrant, orange. "Ah," she said, her heart bursting with joy. "That's better."

Next she said, "I made the earth and sky, and they are serious and important, but I think I'll just play around with them for the fun of it." So she rubbed them together and bounced them around and suddenly there were clouds in all kinds of funny shapes and little tiny motes of earth floating in the air and snowflakes in a million jillion beautiful designs. "Ah," she said, with a joyful smile. "That's better."

Then she said, "I made the plants and animals, and they are serious and important, but I think I'll just play around with them for the fun of it." So she divided them up and put them together again, and suddenly there was silky milkweed that could fly through the air and frogs that went *rib-bit* and monkeys that could swing by their tails. "Ah," she cried, clapping her hands with joy. "That's better."

Finally she said, "I made the humans, and they are serious and important, but I think I'll just play around with them, too, just for the fun of it." So she mixed and matched them, and bounced and tossed them, and divided them and put them together again, and suddenly there were tickly feelings on the bottom of feet and giggles and hugs. "Ah," she said, laughing with joy. "That's much better."

She was having such a good time that she kept right on making all sorts of things just for the fun of it. She kept right on making things that gave her joy.

After all this fun she looked again at her companions, the people, and saw that they were busy working to help her just as she had planned. But to her surprise she saw that they were so busy working on the serious important things that when they walked by flowers and plants, they didn't even see the yellows, reds, or oranges, and when snowflakes fell they didn't look at the patterns, and when frogs went *rib-bit* they didn't hear them. And they hardly ever giggled.

"Wait a minute," she said to herself. "This isn't right. Yes, I want the people to help me, but I also want them to feel the joy in all the things I have made. I want them to have fun, too."

So she called them together and said, "I love you and thank you for all the serious and important work you do to help me. But I have also made lots of things that are for fun. I want you to feel joy in all these wonderful things, just as I do. That is important, too."

After that, when the people saw the orange of a marigold, they stopped and looked at it and felt joy. When snowflakes fell, they got out their magnifying glasses and looked at the patterns and felt joy. When frogs went *rib-bit*, they listened and felt joy. And they tickled and giggled and hugged. The people felt the joy in all the things that God had made.

THE MYSTERY OF GOD

One time when the children were playing hide-and-seek with God, one of them found God hiding in the wind and another found God hiding in some beautiful music and several found God hiding in people who were building a house for people with no home. But when the game was over, they began to want something different.

One of the children said, "We find God in all these different places, but I don't want to see just a part of God. I want to see all of God, all at once!"

The other children agreed. They called to God, saying, "God, the next time you hide and we find you, we want to find all of you, all at once. We want to see everything."

Surprised to hear their request, God said to them, "That isn't as easy as you might think. Let me think about it for a little while." So God thought, "They don't know yet that even though they can know some things about me, they can never know all of me, all at once. Why, even I don't know all of me, all at once. Sometimes, I even surprise myself. How can I help them to understand this?" And God thought and thought some more.

After a while God got an idea. Calling to the children, God said, "All right, I will hide again and this time when you find me, you will find all of me, all at once. But be prepared for a surprise!"

The children jumped up and down, they were so excited. One said, "I think God will be something like the sky at night, with all kinds of shining lights." Another said, "I think God will be like the earth, with everything growing out of it." And a third child said, "Maybe God will be like a person you can talk to." But one child reminded them, "Don't forget, God said, 'Be prepared for a surprise,' so maybe God won't be like any of those things."

Then God said, "I'm ready to hide now. Close your eyes and count to ten."

So the children did and then they went to seek God, this time staying together. They looked and looked but didn't find anything for quite a while, until finally they discovered a box all wrapped up like a present. They looked at each other and said, "Could this be God?" "Should we open it?" And finally they agreed that they should. Very carefully they took off the ribbon, and very carefully they removed the paper, and then very carefully they opened the box and peeked inside.

What they saw did surprise them! It looked like lots and lots of puzzle pieces. Then they heard God say, "Put me together and then you will see all of me, all at once."

So the children began to work, and everyone helped. One piece was a loving heart, and they started with that. Next to it fitted a piece that gave forth a peaceful, quiet feeling, and next to that fitted a family sharing with others. Once they got the first pieces going, it became easier and they began to work faster. They found where the new growth of spring went and where a powerful thunderstorm went. And they did find a person and the sky and the earth, though they were only parts. They worked and worked, putting in more and more of the pieces until they had put in a great number of the pieces. Then they looked to see what pieces they had left, and they were really surprised. The pieces that were left were empty. They fit in, but they weren't anything.

Then they said to God, "Is this truly all of you, all at once?" And God said, "Yes."

One child said, "But there are some pieces where we still don't see you."

"That's true," said God. "Those pieces are where my mystery is."

"Your mystery?"

"You see," God said. "There is much of me that you can see but there is always a part of me that is a mystery. That is where my wonders and surprises come from."

The children stood quietly for a few minutes, looking at the finished puzzle with the places where the mystery was, and they knew that they knew something wonderful.

Then they said to God, "Okay, I guess we're ready to play hide-and-seek again, the old way. Will you hide for us?"

"Off I go!" said God. And they knew that they were going to be surprised once again.

DIFFERENT POINTS OF VIEW

Once upon a time, the children were at the beach playing in the sand. They were digging and patting and talking, making special places. They talked about all kinds of things. They talked about what their special places were like, they talked about what they might have for lunch, and they talked about where the sand came from.

One child said, "The sand came from bigger rocks. The waves kept bumping into the rocks and the rocks got smaller and pretty soon they were sand."

Another child said, "Yes, but God put all those rocks there in the first place. God made the sand." Another child said, "I don't think it was God. I think a long, long time ago there was a great big explosion in space and everything blew out from it."

The children went on and on telling each other what their different ideas were. One child said, "I don't know what to think. I wonder who is right."

"Yeah," the other children agreed. "Who is right?"

Just then they looked up and saw someone coming onto the beach. The person looked sort of like a magician, and she was carrying bags with mysterious objects poking out of them. The children jumped up from the sand and ran to see what this strange person was doing. The woman came over near where the children were playing and set down her bags. Then she took the objects out of the bags and set them up in the sand. They looked sort of like telescopes, but she pointed them at the sand, not up at the sky. Then she said, "These are my Pointing Viewers. Would you like to look through them?"

The children were all excited and said, "Yes, of course we would!"

The magician said, "Now, notice that all the Pointing Viewers are pointed at the same place in the sand, but you must look through each one and remember what you see." They all started looking. Each child looked through each viewer.

"Well, what did you see?" the magician asked them.

"In this one we saw us making special places in the sand."

"In that one we saw the rocks and waves bumping into each other and tiny pieces of sand breaking off."

"In that one over there we saw God making the sand."

"And in this other one we saw a big explosion shooting out the earth and rocks and sand."

"You see something different from each of the viewers," puzzled one of the children. "But how could we? We were always looking at the same thing."

"That's the magic of the Pointing Viewers," said the magician. "You were looking at the same thing, but what you really saw depended on which viewer you looked through. Do you know that your minds are a lot like my Pointing Viewers? You can use your minds to see things like the sand in different ways. And here's the best part! It doesn't mean that one way is right and the other is wrong. Depending on which Pointing Viewer you use, the sand can be made by God or waves or a big explosion and all of those views can be right."

"We're *all* right!" the children yelled. "We're *all* right!!" And the magician picked up her Pointing Viewers, put them back in the bags, and was gone in an instant. The children ran back to their sand creations and went back to digging and patting and talking and sharing their different points of view.

People Have Different Ideas About God

When people wonder about God, they often like to ask other people what they think about God. Usually, the more people they ask, the more ideas about God they will hear. Sometimes they talk to people who don't use the word "God" at all. Instead, those people might say "Spirit" or "Goddess" or "All That Is." Hearing all of these differences is not a problem for people who understand that there are great mysteries in life and no one person can understand them all.

We need each other's help as we try to understand life's mysteries. Here are some ideas about God from four different people. But remember, there are many more ideas.

The first idea about God comes from a woman. Here is what she said:

"Most of the time I'm not really sure, but every once in a while when I'm in my garden, I have a feeling that I do know what God is. When I'm down on my knees digging in the earth, putting tiny seeds into the ground, and when I'm closing the earth over those seeds, knowing that they'll grow into beautiful plants, I feel so amazed that something like that can happen. I just can't imagine what it is that makes those plants grow that way. I think that must be what God is."

The second idea comes from a man. This is what he said:

"Well, it might be easier to tell you what I *don't* think God is. I don't think God is a man with a long beard, sitting up on a cloud, who tells us what we should do and not do. But if I have to say what I think God is, well, let's see, how can I put it? I think God is like the fiery yellow-orange-red power that comes out of the big explosion they call the Big Bang that happened at the beginning of the world. I think that power traveled out into space and slowly over the years became all the things in the universe, even you and me. It's in everything, even the things that we think are bad. I guess that's what I think God is."

The third idea comes from another woman. She said:

"I think God is love. I think of God as being in people's hearts whenever they are caring about other people and trying to help those who need help. If I were to draw a picture of God, I would draw a circle of people all holding hands and I would put a picture of a big

44

red heart on each person. I would put a smile on the face of each person, a smile that shows that they are happy and feeling peaceful. That's my idea of what God is—the love that people have for each other."

Another man said:

"To tell you about my idea, I need to tell about something that happened to me when I was five years old. One day, I couldn't find anyone to play with; everyone was playing with someone else. I wandered alone in the field of grasses and flowers behind our house, feeling lonely and unloved. Suddenly I saw everything was glowing in a great brightness. The flowers and grasses seemed alive with light and warmth and love! I knew that I was a part of All That Is, and I knew that I was loved. I suppose some people would say this is my idea of God, but I don't use the word 'God' when I talk about it."

SEEING GOD WITH AN INNER EYE

Once there was a child who wanted to see God. She said to one of her friends, "I want to see God. Do you know where I can see God?"

Her friend said, "I heard some people say that God is in the earth. Why don't you look at the earth?"

So the child went outside and sat down on some rocks. She looked at the earth all around her. While she was looking she saw a chipmunk come and carry away a seed, and she saw a cat hiding in the leafy shadows of trees. But after she had looked for some time she said, "I don't see God."

So she went to another friend and said, "I want to see God. Do you know where I can see God?"

That friend told her, "I heard some people saying that God is in heaven. Why don't you look in the sky?"

So the child lay down on the earth and looked up at the sky. While she was looking she saw clouds and sunshine, and as day turned to night she saw stars and the moon. But after she had looked all that time she said, "I still don't see God."

So she went to a third friend and said, "I want to see God. Do you know where I can see God?"

Her friend said, "I heard some people say that building down the street is the house of God. Why don't you look there?"

So she went to that building and went inside and looked all around. She saw candles glimmering, and people sitting quietly in the silence, and other people bringing cans of food for hungry people. But after she had looked all around, she said, "I still don't see God." So she went back home, saying to herself, "I don't think you can see God. God must be invisible."

A few nights later, while she was sleeping, she heard a voice as she dreamed. The voice said, "Are you the child who wants to see God?"

"Yes, I am," she said in her dream. "But I've already looked everywhere."

"Well," the voice replied. "Maybe it isn't where you looked but how you looked."

"What do you mean?"

"Well, did you use your ordinary eyes or did you use your inner eye?"

"I—I guess I used my ordinary eyes. What's an inner eye? I don't think I have one."

"Oh, yes, you do," the voice explained, "everyone has an inner eye. You just need to learn how to use it."

"Where is my inner eye?" the child asked.

"Some people say it is where your heart is. And some people say it is in your mind. Others say it is the eye you see with in your dreams. Each of us has to find out for ourselves where our inner eye is. But everyone has one if they just take time to find it."

"Will I really see God if I use my inner eye?" the child asked.

"Try it and see," said the voice. And then all was quiet.

The next day, the child eagerly got up and set out once again to see God. She went outside and again sat on the earth. She closed her ordinary eyes and concentrated on seeing the earth with her inner eye. After a while she saw God in the rocks and the plants and the animals.

Then she lay down and looked up at the heavens. Again she closed her ordinary eyes and concentrated on seeing the heavens with her inner eye. And she saw God in the clouds and sun and the moon and the stars.

Again she walked to the house of God and went in. She sat quietly and closed her ordinary eyes and concentrated on seeing the house of God with her inner eye. She saw that God was in the quiet and in the love of the people.

"I do have an inner eye," the girl said happily to herself. "Now I can see God in the earth and in the skies and in the quiet and in the love of people. God is in everything. I can see God in everything when I see with my inner eye."

GOD IS IN ALL BEINGS OF THE EARTH AND SKY

Behold!   A sacred voice is calling you!
              All over the sky a sacred voice is calling!

This we know:
    all things
    are the work of the Great Mysterious
This we know:
    the Great Mysterious
    is in all things.

Look to the East,
    find the Great Mysterious in the East:

in the mouse
who teaches us that the small can be wise;
in the eagle
who teaches us to be brave;
in the sun
who teaches us to bring light to others.
Look to the East,
    find the Great Mysterious in the yellow of the East.

Look to the South,
    find the Great Mysterious in the South:
in the rose bush
who protects her beauty with thorns;
in the cougar
who notices everything;
in the willow tree
who knows how to bend with the wind.
Look to the South,
    find the Great Mysterious in the red of the South.

Look to the West,
    find the Great Mysterious in the West:
in the power of thunder and lightning;
in the strength of the bear;
in the steady going forward of the turtle.

Look to the West,
    find the Great Mysterious in the brown of the West.

Look to the North,
    find the Great Mysterious in the North:
    in the calmness of the buffalo;
    in the openness of the mountaintop;
    in the peace of the quiet lake.
Look to the North,
    find the Great Mysterious in the white of the North.

This we know:
    all things
    are the work of the Great Mysterious.
This we know:
    the Great Mysterious
    is in all things.

FINDING GOD IN SILENCE

Once there was a man who wanted to know what God was truly like. Other people had told him about God, and he had many ideas himself, but he wanted to see what God would tell him. So he set off to find God.

He searched and searched. Finally he thought he had found God. He said, "God, I want to be sure I know what you are truly like? Some people say you are like a woman and some people say you are like a man. Other people say you are like the sky and yet others say you are like the earth. What are you truly like? Will you tell me, God?"

But God did not speak. God was silent.

So the man went on speaking. "Some people say you are in animals and trees and mountaintops. Other people say you are in the sun and the moon and the stars. What are you truly like? Will you tell me, God?"

But God did not speak. God was silent.

Again the man spoke: "Well, I think you are there in all these things, in earth and sky and animals and people. And I even think you are in me, too. God, why aren't you answering me? God, why don't you tell me what you truly are?"

But still God did not speak. Still God was silent.

Finally the man stopped talking. He waited to hear what God would say. At first he only heard his own words blowing through his mind like a strong wind: "Man—woman—sky—earth." The words blew around and around and the man waited, but God said nothing.

Then the wind grew stronger and the words began to break into little pieces and fall away from him: "M—an, wo—m—an, s—k—y, ear—th." More and more the words broke up and fell away. The man waited and God still said nothing.

When the words were all gone, the man still waited, but God said nothing. And then there was only silence, a calm and peaceful silence, and in the silence he knew God.

◬

GOD IS LIKE LIGHT

This story contains suggestions in brackets for the reader to pause and ask for interaction from the children.

A long time ago, as long ago as could be possible, God was resting. For some time this went on, but finally the time came when God was tired of being still. The Power of God wanted to do something, though it wasn't sure what.

What do you do when you have had enough of resting? [Let the children share ideas.] Well, what God's Power did was to explode itself outwards to see what it would become.

When this explosion happened, God was amazed to find that it shone forth as Light. "Why, I am the Light of the World," it beamed forth. Because God was so full of joy to discover that it could be Light, do you know what God's Power did? [Give the children a chance to guess.] It began to play.

First, it turned itself into trillions of tiny little bits of light that floated in space. But the sparks didn't like being lonely sparks, so they found other sparks to play with, and they made up all sorts of games: ring around the rosie, tag, and hide-and-seek.

As the sparks chased each other and hid and found each other, they began to create beautiful designs. Seeing how lovely these small designs were, God's Power felt the desire to pull them together into larger and larger ones, and it began to dance with arms stretched out wide. It swirled and whirled here, and it twirled and curled there. It charmed together some sparks and chased off others and before long, its dance had gathered the pieces of light together into great spirals of light.

After doing this, the Power of God was ready to do something different again—but what? While it had been playing and dancing, it had noticed that although most of the time it was white, occasionally it seemed to have a little red or a bit of blue or a tinge of yellow. "I wonder if I am any other colors?" the Power of God thought, and then it began to play around with its colors.

First it moved red close to yellow, and there between them glowed an interesting orange. Next it looked closer to see if there was something between yellow and blue and, lo and behold, it saw a glistening green. It checked to see what was between blue and red, and there was a pulsating purple. In between those colors were even more colors. The Power of God was thrilled to find it could be so many shimmering shades.

[Use a prism to cast light around the room.]

To celebrate the many wonders of Light, God lined all the colors up in a row, with red at one end and purple at the other. God then stretched the colors out long and thin, and curved them across the sky in a rainbow so that whenever the people of the earth saw it, they would remember the wonderful Power of God.

God Is Like Darkness

This story contains suggestions in brackets for the reader to pause and ask for interaction from the children.

In the beginning, at the same time when the Power of God took the form of Light, it also took the form of Darkness. Though it may sound strange, whenever it was Light, it was Darkness, too. The two always went together. At first, however, God's Power was so dazzled by its Light that it didn't even notice the Darkness.

After the Power of God had all the fun of seeing what its Light could do, it noticed that whenever it was flickering or flashing or beaming or blazing there was the Darkness in the background, like an empty paper for it to make pictures on. It had been so busy making patterns and designs and turning itself into colors, it hadn't even noticed that no one could see its creations without the Darkness that was always behind and under and around all the brightness of the Light. When it realized this, the Light switched itself off for the moment and decided to find out more about being Darkness. And so it did.

Years later, there was a child and that child's parents had just said, "Time to go to bed."

The child said, "I can't go yet because I have to get a drink of water." But do you know why that child really didn't want to go to bed? [Ask the children for ideas. If they say "afraid of the dark," then say: "That's right, the child was afraid of the darkness." If no one suggests it, just explain that the child was afraid of the darkness.]

The child's parents said, "OK, one quick drink of water and then off to bed." So the child went to bed, and the parents gave one more hug, and then turned off the light.

Lying in bed, the child said, "Why does it have to be dark? Why couldn't it always be light? I don't like this darkness. Why is there darkness, anyway?"

The Power of God that was Darkness heard the child's questions and answered, "Once upon a time I wondered about that very same question, and now I think I understand. If you'd like me to, I could tell you about some of my ideas. Tell me first, though, what is it you don't like about my darkness?"

"Well," said the child, "I can't see anything."

"Yes, in one way that's true," replied the Great Darkness, "but, in another way, it isn't. You can't see things like your toys or your bed, but you can close your eyes and see with your inner eye because those other things aren't getting in the way. You have a chance to see things in your mind and in your spirit, the kind of things that we see in our dreams. You must use your inner eye if your spirit is to grow."

"But sometimes the things I see that way are scary."

"Yes, sometimes they are. But we need to know about the things that scare us so that we can understand them better and so we aren't afraid of them in the daylight. My Darkness gives you a chance to grow stronger and braver in your dreams. And, of course, some dreams are fun or wonderful, too."

"I know," said the child, remembering one very good dream. "But there's another thing I don't like about your Darkness. I can't find my way. If I have to get up I might bump into something and hurt myself."

"Well, if you have to get up and move around, then maybe you do need some light," said the Great Darkness. "But my Darkness comes in the nighttime, and that is the time for resting and not moving. You use up a lot of your power and energy in the daylight, so you need the quiet time of the night to create more energy. That's when you grow. You know how bulbs and seeds need to snuggle into the darkness of the earth before they can grow. And you know how baby animals are in the darkness of eggs or their mothers' wombs before they can be born. All creatures—plants, animals, and people—need both times for moving around and doing things and times for resting and growing."

"Well, maybe darkness is good for those night things," the child admitted. "But when I'm in the dark, sometimes I feel all alone."

"Yes, sometimes we do feel alone, but the people you love are really quite near you, just in the next room," comforted God. "And I am always with you. Darkness is just one of my many forms."

"Well, I guess there is something good about darkness," yawned the child, turning over and curling up like a baby in the dark of its mother's womb. "At least you don't seem too scary when I'm talking to you like this." Then the child's eyes closed and the Darkness that was one of the forms of God wrapped itself very carefully and very gently all around the child. And within the mystery of that Darkness, something new and wonderful began to come to be.

MAKING GOOD THINGS HAPPEN

One day it started to rain. Everyone was glad because they needed water to help the crops grow. It was all right when it rained the next day and the next, but when it kept on raining, people began to be tired of it. When they had to cancel the carnival, the children were very unhappy. "Why does it have to be raining so much?" they said. "Why does God let such a bad thing happen?"

During the next week, it still rained a lot. The children had to stay inside most of the time. They got tired of rainy-day games and they were fussy with each other. Their parents were fussy, too. One day, when they thought they were finally going to get out of the house and go to the carnival, the roads were flooded and they couldn't go.

"Why, oh why, is it raining so much?" they asked. "Why doesn't God make it stop?"

Later, they watched TV and saw that the rains had filled up the rivers so that they were flowing over their banks and water was coming into the houses of people who lived near the rivers. They also heard that those people had to leave their houses and go live at the school because it wasn't safe for them to stay in their homes anymore. "How terrible! Those poor people!" the children said. "Why does God let such bad things happen?"

"Maybe God hasn't noticed how much rain has fallen. Maybe God doesn't know how bad it is," the children said. "Maybe we should talk to God."

So the children did. "Hi, God, we need to talk to you. There's been an awful lot of rain here lately," one of them said.

"God, it's really too much rain. The streets are flooded, the rivers are overflowing, and we can't go outside," said another.

"Can't you do something about all this rain? Why do you let these bad things happen?" asked a third child.

"Don't you even care?" asked a fourth.

They waited to hear what God would say.

Finally, God answered them. "Hi, children, here I am. Yes, I do know that there's been a lot of rain and that it's causing problems, and yes, I do care. But, you see, things like the rain in your town are only one part of all the things in the Great Big Universe. If you could see the Great Big Universe with my God's eyes, you would see how this 'too much rain' in your town is just one part of the whole picture. If you could see the Great Big Universe with my God's eyes, you would see that it isn't always easy to know what is good and what is bad. If you could see the Great Big Universe with my God's eyes, you would see that because there is freedom in the world, things can sometimes surprise even me."

"But we don't like it that we can't go out to play!"

"When we tried to go to the carnival the roads were flooded!"

"It's terrible that the people near the rivers have to leave their houses!"

"Something should be done about it!" said one child after the other.

"Yes, it should," said God, "but you are forgetting something."

"What?" the children asked.

"The work of the world is too much for me alone. I have to keep a watch on the whole Great Big Universe with my God's eyes, but I need you to help me when there are difficulties in your part of that great big world."

"But what can we do?" asked the children. "We can't make the rain stop."

"No," said God, "but you can help the people who had to leave their houses."

"I guess we could," the children said.

And so they did. They talked to their parents, and they found extra cots and blankets. They gathered up extra clothing. They made muffins and casseroles. They chose lots of their rainy-day games and their musical instruments, and they took them down to the school to share with the people whose houses had been flooded. They stayed a while and played games with the children who were there, and they sang songs together. As they were singing "You Are My Sunshine," the rain stopped and the sun came out again.

Then God said to the children, "The world I have created is full of many things and there are mysteries that are not easy to understand, but you have made good things happen in your part of the Great Big Universe. Thank you for helping me."

The children said, "You are welcome! We like helping and we want to do it again."

"I'm sure you will," said God.

Everflowing Forgiveness

Once there was a man who had many friends. He liked to be with his friends, to talk with them and to play with them, and even to work with them. He also liked to talk to God.

One day this man went off to meet with one of his friends. He was feeling happy because he and his friend had decided to work together to help a family repair their house. The two friends sat down to talk over their ideas, but very quickly things seemed to go wrong.

The man had one idea but his friend said, "Your idea won't work. I have a better idea." But after the friend shared his idea, the man said, "Your idea is the one that won't work. My idea was better." The friend said, "You always think your ideas are best." And the man said, "You never even listen to my ideas."

Before long they were really arguing and the friend said, "I don't know why I ever wanted to work with you. You are just plain stubborn!" And the man said, "Good, because I don't want to work with you either. You don't think I'm good enough. You're stuck-up!" And they each went home full of hurt and anger.

A week went by, and it was a terrible week. At the end of the week the man said to himself, "I really feel bad. I miss my friend, but when I remember what he said, I'm still mad. What can I do to make things better?" Then he remembered that sometimes it helped him to share his problems with God. So the man said to God, "Last week I had an argument with my friend and I'm still feeling bad about it. What can I do to make it better?"

God said, "Close your eyes for a minute and imagine you can see the whole universe. Now imagine that you are seeing people in the universe having arguments. Now look again and see if you can imagine a golden light. That is the everflowing golden light of forgiveness. In your mind, see the people who are having arguments moving into the golden light. As they do, they are saying to each other, 'I'm sorry I hurt you and I forgive you for hurting me.' Forgiveness is always there. If you can forgive each other, you and your friend will feel better."

"I don't know if I can," the man said. "He really hurt me."

"I know that you were hurt, but have you thought about how your friend is feeling?" God asked.

"Well," replied the man, "Maybe I said some things that hurt him.

I suppose he might be feeling bad, too."

Then the man realized how much he wanted to be friends again. He went to find his friend and said, "I'm sorry if I said something that hurt you, and I forgive you for saying things that hurt me. I miss you and I want to be friends again." And guess what! The man's friend said the same thing back to him.

Then the man heard God whispering inside him, "Do you see the golden light? Do you feel the golden warmth?" The man closed his eyes again. He began to see the golden light swirling all around them, and he felt its warmth. "This is the light of everflowing forgiveness," God whispered. "It is always there for those who know the secret mystery of it."

"What is the mystery?" the man wanted to know.

"The mystery is: When you forgive others, you also are forgiven."

Soon the man realized that he was no longer feeling bad, but that he was now happy. Before long the two friends were busily working again to repair the house.

▲

GOD CREATES AND NAMES

In the beginning God created the heavens and the earth. Nothing had a shape yet, and everywhere it was dark and watery. But in this empty, watery darkness, the Spirit of God was stirring.

Then God spoke, saying "Let there be light!" And there was light, and God saw that the light was good. Then God separated the light from the darkness and God called the light Day and the darkness Night. And there was evening and morning, one day.

God spoke again, saying, "Let there be a divider placed to separate the waters above that rain down on us from the waters down below." And it was so. God called the divider Sky. And there was evening and morning, a second day.

God said, "Let the waters under the Sky be gathered together and let the dry land appear." And it was so. God called the dry land Earth, and the waters were called Seas. And God saw that it was good. Then God said, "Let the earth put forth plants and fruit trees with seeds in them to make more plants and trees." And it was so. God saw that it was good, and there was evening and morning, a third day.

God said, "Let there be lights up in the sky to tell when it is day and when it is night. And let the lights tell us the seasons and the days and the years." And it was so. So God made the two great lights, the Sun to tell when it is day and the Moon to tell when it is night. God saw that it was good, and there was evening and morning, a fourth day.

God said, "Let the waters bring forth swarms of living creatures, and let birds fly above the earth across the sky." So God created all the creatures that swim in the seas, and every bird that flies in the skies, and God saw that it was good. God blessed them saying, "Be fruitful and multiply and fill the seas and the earth." And there was evening and morning, a fifth day.

Then God said, "Let there be all kinds of living creatures to move upon the earth: cattle, creeping things, and wild animals." And it was so.

"Now," said God. "I will make human beings created in my image." So God created humans, both female and male. God blessed them and said to them, "Be fruitful and multiply, and fill the earth. You are responsible for the earth, and the fish, and the birds, and every living thing that moves upon the earth. I have given you this earth with plants and trees, and I have given the beasts and the birds and the creeping things green plants to eat." And it was so. God saw everything that was made and, behold, it was very good. And there was evening and morning, a sixth day.

The heavens and the earth were finished, and on the seventh day God rested from all the work. So God blessed the seventh day and made it holy, because on that day God finished creating and rested. This is the story of how God created the heavens and the earth.

MOTHER MAWU WANTS PEACE

In the beginning, Mawu, Mother of All, made the sky and the earth. Way up in the sky, she hung the fiery sun. Then she called her Rainbow Colored Serpent to her and she climbed into his mouth. Together they pushed up the mountains and carved out the valleys. She started the shining rivers winding their way down from the mountaintops and through the valleys. And the sky and the earth and the mountains and the rivers were a part of her because she carved them out.

And in the beginning Mawu, Mother of All, made the animals. She took the clay of the earth and patted it and rolled it. In her mind she imagined all kinds of designs. There were long-legged giraffes and leaping gazelles. There were huge whales and tiny hummingbirds. She molded the clay into the shape of all the animals, and the animals were a part of her because she molded them.

And in the beginning Mawu, Mother of All, made people. She took some of the animals and had them stand up on two legs so that they could use their hands for all kinds of clever things. And when she finished the people, she breathed her own breath-spirit into them and gave them life. And the people were a part of her because they had Mother Mawu's breath-spirit in them.

And in the beginning Mawu said to her people, "I have breathed my breath-spirit into you, and because my breath is in each one of you, you must care for each other just as if you were caring for me. Go now and live together happily and in peace."

Now Mawu had a holy daughter named Gbadu. When Mawu was finished with all her creating, she left Gbadu to watch over the people. For a while the people lived in peace and they were happy. But as time went by, they began to forget what their Mother Mawu had told them. When Gbadu looked out over the people, she saw that the people were fighting and she saw much sadness.

Gbadu decided something had to be done. She called her own children together and she said to them, "Your Grandmother Mawu gave each of the people her breath-spirit, and she wanted them to be happy and to live in peace. But look! They are fighting all the time and there is much sadness. You must go and teach them again how to live in peace."

So Mawu's grandchildren went out over the earth to teach the people how to live in peace. Everywhere they went they gathered groups of people together and said to them, "Remember, it was Mawu who put her breath-spirit in you. Remember that because Mawu's spirit is in each one of you, if you fight with another person you are fighting with Mawu. Don't you know your Mother Mawu wants you to live in peace with each other?"

Some of the time the people remember, and then they live in peace. But sometimes they forget, and when they do they fight with each other. When this happens it is time again for someone to remind the people that the breath-spirit of Mawu, the Mother of All, is in each person, and because of that they must care for each other as if they were caring for Mawu. When the people remember this, they will be happy and they will live in peace.

MANY PATHS TO GOD

Once upon a time, five travelers from different lands met near a mountain. These travelers had been told that if they climbed the mountain, they would find God at the top. Around the bottom of the mountain there were many paths to choose from. The travelers had been told beforehand which of the paths to take, and they also had been told that only that path would bring them to God.

The travelers met each other at the bottom of the mountain and told each other of their search for God.

The first traveler said, "I am trying to find God. I have been told that of all these paths the right path to take is that one, the flowery meadow path. I have been told that if I follow it, at the top I will find God, the Great Mother of All."

The second traveler said, "That's interesting. I have been told that the right path to take is that steep, cliffside path over there, and if I follow it, at the top I will find God, the Great Father in Heaven."

The third traveler said, "Strange that we have all been told to follow different paths. I have been told that the right path is that wide river valley path, and if I follow it, at the top I will find God, the Great Spirit in All Things."

The fourth traveler said, "Yes, this is strange. I have been told to follow even a different path. My path is the deep forest path, and I'm told if I follow it, at the top I will find God, the Great Peaceful Silence."

Finally the fifth traveler spoke, saying, "And I have been told something different from all of you—that the right path is the path with a view of the sea, and if I follow it, at the top I will find God, the Great One Who Loves Us All."

The travelers were surprised to hear about the other paths, because they were sure that the path they had been told to follow was the only right one. They even tried to convince the others to follow their chosen path, saying such things as:

"I'm sure my way is the right one."

"Change your minds and come my way."

"Don't you think it would be best for you to come this way?"

But none would change.

So, bidding each other good-bye, they began their journeys to the top. As they started out each was singing a song of praise to God.

They could hear each other's songs in the distance and they thought to themselves, "How very strange those other songs sound!" But off they went on their chosen paths. They soon were traveling alone and could no longer hear any of the others. Sometimes following the path was easy and sometimes it was hard.

Finally, each of the five travelers neared the top of the mountain. They began to hear the other travelers' songs once again, but now they said to themselves, "I didn't realize before how beautiful those songs are." All five came to the top within minutes of each other. They stopped and eagerly looked around.

The first called out, "Oh, Great Mother of All, I have found you!"

The second called out, "Oh, Great Father in Heaven, I have found you!"

The third called out, "Oh, Great Spirit in All Things, I have found you!"

The fourth called out, "Oh, Great Peaceful Silence, I have found you!"

The fifth called out, "Oh, Great One Who Loves Us All, I have found you!"

But all of them were seeing and calling out to the same God.

Then they realized that they had all been searching for the same thing, though each had called it by a different name and each had taken a different path. At this, they reached out for each other's hands, formed a circle right there on the top of the mountain, and began to sing again. And now, as each of them sang their songs, there seemed to be only one song—a joyous song of love for God.

GOD COMES TO US IN OUR DREAMS

There once was a girl who lived with her family in a small village. It was a very small village, so everyone there knew each other. The girl's family loved her and the people of the village loved her. When she woke up crying one night because she had had a frightening dream, everyone in the village knew about it and everyone cared.

In the morning, the people of the village asked the girl about her scary dream. "In my dream, I was walking down the path to get some wood," she recalled. "All of a sudden a tiger jumped down from a tree and got in front of me on the path so I couldn't go by." The girl almost started to cry again as she remembered how scary it was. "Then the tiger started coming toward me and it was snarling and growling and showing its teeth, and I was sure it wanted to eat me. I turned around and started to run as fast as I could, but the tiger ran right behind me. Just as it was going to catch me with one of its huge paws, I woke up!" The girl went to her mother and hid her head under her mother's arm. She was still very frightened when she thought of the dream, and she was afraid for night to come when she would have to sleep again.

The elders in the village gathered together and talked for a while about the girl's dream. Then they went back to the girl, who was still with her mother, and said, "If you want to learn not to be afraid in your dreams, we can help you."

The girl thought for a minute and then said, very quietly, "I do want to learn not to be afraid in my dreams."

One of the elders said to her, "All right then, try this: Tonight if you dream the same dream and the tiger starts to come toward you, don't run, but stay where you are and say 'Hello, tiger.'"

"But the tiger will eat me," said the girl. "I'm too scared."

"Yes, you may be scared," replied the elders, "but we believe you will be brave enough to do it. And we don't think the tiger will eat you."

That night the girl dreamed of the tiger again. But when the tiger started toward her, she remembered and stood bravely, facing the tiger, and said, "Hello, tiger." When the tiger got right in front of her, it stopped.

And then a wonderful thing happened. As the girl looked at the tiger's face, she saw it smile, and as she looked some more, the tiger's face began to change and she saw there the faces of lots of animals. They smiled at her, too. As she looked some more, the animals' faces changed into faces of people, and the people's faces smiled at her. The girl felt a wonderful happy feeling coming over her when she realized that she wasn't afraid anymore. And then, as she looked again, she saw not only the animals and the people, but trees and earth and sky and water and beautiful colors and beautiful darkness all swirling around and mixing together, and all smiling at her. And she felt a great joy.

The next morning the girl couldn't wait to tell everyone in the village about her dream. Everyone gathered around, and as she told it, everyone sighed and smiled and shared her joy. Once again the elders went off by themselves for a while to talk about the girl's dream. When they returned one of the elders said to her, "You were blessed, my daughter. Because you were brave, God has come to you in your dream and blessed you."

Later that day, as the girl was walking down the path to get some wood, she was still thinking about her wonderful dream. She was eager for night to come so that she could dream again.

▲

CHANGING WOMAN, CHANGING WORLD

A long, long time ago, nothing changed. People were not young and old; they just were. Days didn't have morning and evening; they just were. Years didn't have summer and winter; they just were. In that time, nothing changed.

Then one day Changing Woman, one of the Holy Ones, appeared as a baby on the top of a mountain. It was raining and all around her mists swirled. Then sunbeams shone and all around her rainbows glistened. Her carrying cradle was made from the rainbows, with laces from the sun rays and a headpiece from the dark clouds.

Changing Woman changed, and she became a child dressed in clothes made of white shells. After four days Changing Woman changed again, this time into a young maiden, and as a young maiden she wore clothing of turquoise. After four more days Changing Woman changed again, this time into an adult, and as an adult she wore clothing of abalone. And after four more days Changing Woman changed again into an old, old woman, and as an old, old woman she wore clothing of jet-black coal. This is why she is called Changing Woman. And because of Changing Woman all people's lives change from baby to child to teen to adult to elderly person.

Changing Woman stood in her white shell clothing, looking to the east, and when she did, the sun began to rise and it was dawn. Then Changing Woman turned and stood in her turquoise clothing looking to the south, and when she did, the sun rose overhead and it was midday. Then Changing Woman turned and stood in her abalone clothing looking to the west, and when she did, the sun began to set and it was twilight. Then Changing Woman turned and stood in her jet-black coal clothing looking to the north, and when she did, the stars came out and it was night. This is why she is called Changing Woman. And because of Changing Woman each day changes from dawn to midday to twilight to night.

Changing Woman's house was way beyond the sea. It had four rooms. The first room was in the east, decorated with white shells. When Changing Woman went to live in that room it became spring: Tender green grasses poked out of the earth, flowers bloomed, and new baby animals were born.

The second room was in the south, decorated with turquoise. When Changing Woman went to live in that room it became summer:

Corn grew tall, fruit ripened, and animals romped and played.

The third room was in the west, decorated with abalone. When Changing Woman went to live in that room it became autumn: It was time to gather the harvest, and people and animals stored food for coming months.

The fourth room was in the north, decorated with jet-black coal. When Changing Woman went to live in that room it became winter: Plants died, animals hibernated, and it was cold.

But then, after winter, Changing Woman always moved back to the first room—the white shell room, the room of spring—and the seasons began again. That is why she is called Changing Woman. And because of Changing Woman, each year changes from spring to summer to autumn to winter and back to spring again.

When God takes the form of Changing Woman, things are forever changing:

When Changing Woman changes, the times of a person's life change.
When Changing Woman changes, the times of day change.
When Changing Woman changes, the times of year change.

Changing Woman says:
I bless the changes in a person's life.
I bless the changes of the day.
I bless the changes of the year.
I am Changing Woman. I am God. I am here.

The Spirit of God Is There When a Baby Is Born

Once upon a time, an egg from a woman and a sperm from a man came together to create something new. That new beginning nestled into the woman's womb, a special place where babies grow, where it was warm and cozy and safe. In the beginning this small being was very, very tiny; tinier than a little dot. Then it began to grow. As it grew, it changed from the size of a dot to the size of a bean to the size of a hand. Its heart began to beat. And the spirit of God was there in the growing and the changing.

Now the little person began to move around. It was like a little space-being floating in the waters of the woman's womb. It turned its head and swung its arms and kicked its legs and moved from one place to another. One day, this new person gave one of its kicks and the woman could feel it moving. And the spirit of God was there in the moving.

Time went on and the baby grew bigger and bigger. It became more and more the person it was meant to be. It frowned and made all kinds of faces. If it wanted comforting it sucked its thumb. It liked some noises like music, but didn't like others. When the woman was quiet or asleep, the baby was often awake, moving around. And when the woman was awake and walking around, the baby was rocked to sleep. You could begin to see the special, one-of-a-kind person that the baby would be. And the spirit of God was there in the baby's specialness.

Finally the time came near for the baby to be born. It was ready to live outside the woman's body. The woman's body made itself ready for the baby to come out. Her womb muscles pushed and pushed. Sometimes she worked very hard and sometimes she rested. The people who loved her, helped her. And the spirit of God was there in the laboring.

And then the baby was born. It entered the outside world and took its first breath. Loving arms took the baby, wrapped it in blankets, and held it close. And the baby once again felt warm and cozy and safe. All of the people who knew about this baby were full of joy that it was born. They wondered at the mystery of this tiny new person. And the spirit of God was there in the love and the joy and the mystery.

◭

The Spirit of God Is There When Someone Dies

Many years ago a baby was born. As that baby began to breathe for the first time, the spirit of God was in the baby's breathing.

The baby nursed and slept and opened her eyes and nursed and slept some more, and as time went by she could do more things. The baby learned to sit up and to crawl, and soon she learned to walk. Now she could go all over, exploring everything. And the spirit of God was in her exploring.

Soon the baby was a girl who could run and talk and pedal a bike. And the little girl became a bigger girl who went to school and learned to read and write and do arithmetic. She could swim and ride a bicycle and row a boat. She could play a piano. She could make all kinds of things: bird houses, cookies, and gardens. And the spirit of God was in her learning.

Before long the girl was a youth who went to high school. She learned to drive. She began to think about what she would be when she was all grown up and she could decide more things for herself. And the spirit of God was in her deciding.

The girl became a woman. She found work to do and she found people she loved and she had her own home. One day she became a mother and had children of her own. She cared for her children, played with them, and taught them lots of things. She worked to help make the world a better place for all people. And the spirit of God was in her loving.

Time went by and this woman grew older. Her children grew up and they had children, and the woman became a grandmother. The time came when she retired from her work. Then she had more time to do the things she liked to do for fun, like playing with her grandchildren. And the spirit of God was in her playing.

This grandmother grew older and older until she was a very old woman. Some of her grandchildren had children, and she became a great-grandmother. Now she tired more easily and moved more slowly. She couldn't see or hear things as easily as before. And the spirit of God was with her in her aging.

Then this very old woman's body became very tired, and her family knew she was dying. As they went to visit her, they did whatever they could to make her more comfortable. They talked with her about all the wonderful things they remembered doing with her, and they shared their sadness at the thought of losing her. Sometimes the very old woman was sad that she was dying, and sometimes she was glad. And the spirit of God was with her in her dying.

Then the very old woman's breathing became slower and slower, and her breath became softer and softer, and then she breathed her last breath out and she died. And the spirit of God was with her.

Later her friends and relatives came together to share their sadness, and they talked with each other about the things she had said and done in her life. And the spirit of God was in their remembering.

THE HEALING POWER OF GOD

Once a boy went to visit his grandparents. At his grandparents' place there was a tree, and this boy climbed up into the tree just as he had done many times before. But this time, for some reason—maybe it was his smooth-bottomed church shoes—the boy suddenly slipped and fell out of the tree. He fell onto his right elbow, and by the time he was through falling, his arm hurt terribly. It hurt so much he cried.

His family all came running. When they saw his arm they knew something was really wrong, so they quickly took him to the hospital. There the doctor took an x-ray of his arm and found that the elbow joint was twisted out of place. The doctor said, "Don't worry. I can fix it." Soon the joint was back in place and the boy's arm was in a cast.

The doctor said to him, "Your arm is going to be as good as new, but healing takes time. The cast will have to stay on for four weeks." They gave him a sling to help hold up his arm, and the boy went home with his family. When he got home he ate a little bit, but he was so tired and soon went to sleep.

The next day he had to lie still and rest a lot, and his arm still hurt. His family brought him food, and his uncle cut up one of his shirts so it would fit over the cast. Other relatives and friends came by to see him. They told him how sorry they were that he had injured himself, and they tried to amuse him. They brought a balloon that said, "Get well!" And they made cards that said, "We're sorry you fell out of the tree. Get well soon. We love you!" And they brought him some video movies to watch. By the end of the day the boy was feeling better.

As the days went by the boy felt a lot better. His arm didn't hurt any more, and he got pretty good at doing things with his left hand. He even learned to write and draw with his left hand, although he usually used his right one. But he was tired of not having both hands and arms to do things with. He said to his parents, "I'm tired of not being well. I want my arm to get well right away. I want to take off this old cast! When can I take it off?"

His parents said to him, "We know you're getting tired of having the cast on, but healing takes time." They showed him on the calendar how many more days it would be before his arm would be thoroughly healed and the cast could come off.

"That's too long," the boy said. "I want to get well right now!! Maybe God can make me well right now, or at least by tomorrow."

So the boy talked to God. He said, "God, you probably noticed that I fell out of the tree and twisted my elbow out of joint and that the doctor put it back right and that now I have it in a cast. They tell me it'll be lots more days before it's all healed, but I'm tired of having a cast. Couldn't you make it heal faster? Couldn't you make it well right now or at least by tomorrow?" And the boy waited to hear what God would say.

Finally the boy heard God say, "Yes, I know you've hurt your arm and I'm sorry. I know it must be hard to wait for it to thoroughly heal, but taking time is one of the ways that my healing power works."

"What are some of the other ways?" the boy asked, hoping there was a quicker way to get well.

"Well, you've already been using my other ways. You went to the doctor and he used his knowledge of how elbow joints work to get your joint back in place. One of the ways that my healing energy works is with medicines and with doctors' skills."

"What other ways of healing do you have?" the boy wondered.

"Well, tender loving care is another," God said. "And you've been getting that, too. Your family and your friends have been giving you lots of love and care, bringing you good wishes with balloons and cards and videos. My healing energy is in the tender loving care of family and friends. I know it's hard to wait, but you will be well soon."

So the boy said to God, "Okay, I guess I should be glad that you have all those different healing powers. I'm glad to know that my arm will be all well again." And the boy decided to go and draw another of his left-handed pictures.

God Wants Fairness

When God created the world and the people, God saw to it that there was plenty of land and plenty of water and plenty of good things to eat. God saw to it that there were enough good things in the world for everyone. God said, "The world I have created is good. The people I have created are made in my likeness. I have blessed them and given them all they need for a good life." And the people were kind to each other and treated each other fairly. They were glad about the wonderful things in the world and they offered gifts to God. They sang and made music and danced. And God was happy.

But somehow, as time went by, many of the people were no longer content. Even though they had enough to live easily, they began to notice every little difference between what they had and what others had. They spent a lot of time comparing and saying, "This is good! That is bad!" and "That is bad! This is good!" Many people were no longer happy, and God was sad.

It got even worse. Because some of the people wanted what others had, they began to be unfair to each other. Sometimes they told a lie in order to get something they wanted. Sometimes, when they were selling to others, they cheated them. Sometimes they stole. Sometimes they fought and hurt others, and God was very sad.

God tried to tell them to care about each other and to be fair, but they didn't seem to hear God. Then God called to a man named Moses, because God knew that he cared about fairness. God said to him, "Moses, I am going to give my people some laws. These laws will help them to be fair with each other. I want you to go and tell my laws to the people. Maybe they will listen to you."

Moses gathered the people together and said, "Here are some of God's laws: Do not wish for things that belong to others. Do not tell lies. Do not steal. Do not hurt others." Moses went on, "If you obey God's laws you will be fair to each other and you will be happy again." The people seemed to listen and God was hopeful.

For a while it worked. But soon many of the people forgot the laws and began to be unfair again. Because they always wanted more, they were unhappy and God was unhappy. They remembered how God had enjoyed their gifts and music and dances. They thought they might bring cheer to themselves and to God if they sang their songs, played their instruments, and danced, so they brought gifts to God, sang their songs, played their instruments, and danced. But it only made God angry to hear their songs and dances while at the same time they were being unfair to each other.

So God tried again, calling to the shepherd Amos, saying, "Amos, speak these words of mine to the people."

So Amos said, "Here is what God says: I can't enjoy your music and dances and gifts while you are so unfair to each other. Take away the noise of your songs and the melody of your harps. What I want is for fairness to roll down like water; for fairness to be like an everflowing stream."

This time some of the people heard what it was that God really wanted, and they wrote down the words of God that Moses and Amos had spoken. And all through the years and even today, whenever people forget what it is that God wants, the words are there in the Hebrew Bible to read over and over again. And when people are fair and care for each other, then God loves the offerings and the singing and the music and the dancing. When people are fair, God is very, very happy.

◭

LOVE YOUR NEIGHBOR AS YOURSELF

This story contains suggestions in brackets for the reader to pause and ask for interaction from the children.

A long time ago, Jesus walked from village to village talking with the people of Palestine about what God wanted them to do. When he came to a village, women and men, girls and boys would gather around him and listen to his stories and ask him questions.

One day, Jesus was talking with a man who knew a lot about the rules that God wanted the people to follow. Do you remember the rules that God told Moses? [Repeat the rules: don't lie, don't steal, don't hurt others.] This man asked Jesus, "Which is the most important one of the rules—which rule is the greatest?"

Jesus answered him, "The most important rule is to love God, and if you love God, then you will love your neighbor just as you love yourself."

The man thought for a moment and then said, "Well, what do you mean by 'neighbor'? I know I should love my family and I guess I should love the other people in my village. Is that what you mean by 'loving my neighbor'? Or maybe you mean I should love all the people in my country. What do you mean by 'neighbor'?"

"Well," said Jesus. "Let me tell you a story." The people all sat down and got comfortable, because they knew that Jesus' stories were very important and they wanted to listen very carefully.

Jesus started his story: "Once there was a man who went on a trip. As he was walking along, robbers came up to him and took everything he had. They beat him and then they went away, expecting him to die.

"Now by chance a holy man, who was from the same country as the man, came along the road. When he saw the man lying there, he was afraid that the robbers might still be near, so he passed right by him on the other side.

"Soon another important man, a man from the same village, came along in a great hurry, and seeing that the hurt man looked almost dead, he also crossed to the other side of the road and passed by.

"Finally a Samaritan came by. Now Samaritans were people from the north, and the people of Palestine thought they did everything the wrong way. When the Samaritan saw the hurt man lying there, he was moved with pity for him. He bandaged his wounds, then he put him up on his donkey and took him to an inn and took care of him.

"The next day this man from Samaria, the hated country, took out some coins and gave them to the innkeeper, saying, 'Take care of this man. When I come back I will repay you for whatever more you have spent.'"

Then Jesus asked the man who had questioned him, the one who knew a lot about God's rules, "Which of these three people acted like a neighbor to the man who fell into the hands of the robbers?" And the man said, "The third man, the man from Samaria, was the one who acted like a neighbor."

But some of the other people said, "Are you saying that loving your neighbor means loving everybody, not just people in your family or village or country? Do you mean a neighbor is anybody, even someone from a country where they do everything the wrong way?"

Jesus said, "Yes, and I say to you, 'Go, and do likewise.'"

GOD IS IN EACH ONE OF US

This story contains suggestions in brackets for the reader to personalize the tale for the child.

Once there was a boy named Svetaketu (Svay-tah-kay-too) who went away to school to learn all about God. When he came back home, his father could see that although he had learned many things, there were still some things, some very important things, that he did not yet understand. When his father told him that there was more for him to learn, Svetaketu said, "Please, Father, teach me." His father said, "So be it, my son."

Svetaketu's father said, "Go bring me a fig from that large tree over there." Svetaketu ran to pluck a fig and brought it to his father, saying, "Here it is, sir."

His father said, "Cut it in two." Svetaketu cut the fig in two, saying, "I have done as you asked."

Then his father said, "What do you see in the fig?" Svetaketu answered, "All these little tiny seeds."

Then Svetaketu's father said, "Cut one of the tiny seeds in two." And Svetaketu did. Svetaketu's father then asked, "What do you see now?"

Svetaketu answered, "Nothing at all."

Svetaketu's father said, "My son, I want you to know that even though you can't see it, there is an unseen power in that seed. This power can grow such a seed into a great tree like the one over there. And the unseen power that is in the seed is the same power that is in the whole world. That power is God. That power is Spirit, and God's spirit-power is in you, too."

When Svetaketu heard his father's words, he felt both very small and very big to think that such a wonderful power could be in him. He asked his father to teach him more about the spirit-power of God that was in him.

His father did, and Svetaketu learned that even though this spirit-power cannot be seen by our ordinary eyes, we can see it with our inner eye. It is there in such mysteries as growing and loving.

And that spirit-power is in each one of us. It is in everyone here at church. It is in everyone in [your town or area]. It is in everyone in [your state or province]. It is in everyone in [your country]. It is in each and every person in the whole world.

◭

About the Stories

"Hide-and-Seek With God" was inspired by a story in *The Book*, by Alan Watts. That story, in turn, was informed by the Hindu concepts of *lila* (life is like God-play) and *maya* (life is not real in our usual sense of real).

"God Has Many Names" draws on two themes: Islam's ninety-nine names of God, which delineate attributes and qualities of the one God, Allah, and a concern for the equality of male and female images of God.

"The One Great Web of Life" considers the concept of "the interdependent web of all existence of which we are a part," found in Unitarian Universalism's Seventh Principle, as a God image. Native Americans, Hindus, and Buddhists also use the web as an important metaphor for life or God.

"God Is Like the Mother of All" was developed from theories found in cosmology and feminist theology.

"God Is Like a Father" is an imaginative and more elementary version of stories about Jesus' life and teachings found in the Christian Bible.

"Being With God in Prayer" attempts to relate children's questions about prayer to the wisdom of the world's religions about how prayer works.

"God Is Like a Compassionate Deer" is a simplified retelling of the Buddhist Jataka tale called "The Fabulous Sharabha Deer" in *The Marvelous Companion: Life Stories of the Buddha* (a children's version is called *A Precious Life: Jataka Tales Series*). The deer in the story is believed to be the Buddha in a former life.

"Things God Made for Joy" draws on ideas expressed in *The Color Purple* by Alice Walker, and from the Hindu belief that God is *Sat-chit-ananda,* or being-awareness-bliss.

"The Mystery of God" is a follow-up to the first story, "Hide-and-Seek With God," that emphasizes the sense of mystery found in all religions.

"Different Points of View" promotes the underlying themes of all these stories: We each see the world (and God) from unique viewpoints, and the more we are open to the viewpoints of others, the greater our vision of the whole.

"People Have Different Ideas About God" contains imaginative versions of beliefs about God that were expressed by numerous people in workshops on God images.

"Seeing God With an Inner Eye" was created to help young children mediate between their desire for concrete, sensual answers and their intuitive, spiritual abilities. The concept that one can come to know God by use of an inner eye or divine eye is found in many religions, especially in Hinduism.

"God Is In All Beings of the Earth and Sky" is a chant based on words and ideas from Black Elk, Chief Seattle, and the book, *The Sacred Tree,* created by the Four Worlds Development Project in Lethbridge, Alberta, Canada.

"Finding God in Silence" reworks and blends a Zen Buddhist tale with 1 Kings 19:11-12 in the New Revised Standard Version of the Hebrew Bible.

"God Is Like Light" combines the theories of cosmologists and physicists with the visions of a great many of the world's religions.

"God Is Like Darkness" flows from Taoism and the belief that the eternal Tao, or the Way, always reflects a complementary patterning of opposites: If God is like light, then God is also like darkness. It also expresses many children's feelings about the dark.

"Making Good Things Happen" draws from three universal religious concerns: the question, "Why do bad things happen?"; the understanding that some of God's ways are inscrutable to us; and the faith that we can still make good things happen despite such troubling mysteries.

"Everflowing Forgiveness" was inspired by stories of God's forgiveness in the Christian Bible and by a picture of a forgiving Goddess drawn by a ten-year-old girl.

"God Creates and Names" is a retelling of Genesis 1:1-2:4a in the Hebrew Bible.

"Mother Mawu Wants Peace" originates in a story of the Dahomey People of Benin, Africa. Merlin Stone's version of that story, found in *Ancient Mirrors of Womanhood*, inspired and informed this version for children.

"Many Paths to God" was derived from ideas on Hinduism in Huston Smith's *The World's Religions*. Ideas expressed here are also found in the writings of Ramakrishna.

"God Comes to Us in Our Dreams" is fashioned after the Senoi people of Malaysia, who are said to actively influence their children's dreams in a similar manner. The belief that dreams may be communication with God is found in many other religions.

Information about Changing Woman, an important Navajo deity, can be found in the book *Blessingway*, by Leland Wyman.

"The Spirit of God Is There When a Baby Is Born" was inspired by the wonder felt at the birth of a child and by the recognition of this mystery by all religions.

"The Spirit of God Is There When Someone Dies" was inspired by the spiritual power felt at the death of a person and by the recognition of this mystery by all religions. If read to boys, this story can be made more meaningful by changing the baby to a boy instead of a girl.

"The Healing Power of God" draws on the awareness of most religions that God and the power of healing are related. This story identifies attributes of that healing as time, modern medicine, and loving care.

"God Wants Fairness" is a simple condensation of the visions of the prophets in the Hebrew Bible.

"Love Your Neighbor as Yourself" comes from the story found in Luke 10:25-29 of the Christian Bible.

"God Is In Each One of Us" is found in the Hindu Upanishads, Chandogya 6.12.

ABOUT THE AUTHOR

A religious educator for more than 30 years, Mary Ann Moore is the author of the curriculum *Stories About God*, from which these stories are taken. She has written and contributed to numerous Unitarian Universalist curricula for children and adults, including *God Images, Doing Plays With Kids, Timeless Themes* and *World Religions*. She and her husband live in Sudbury, Massachusetts.